I0469042

YouTube Marketing:

Winning an Audience and Making Cash

Brendan Mace

Table of Contents

FREE BONUS: Simple Two Step Formula

Click Here to Get Your FREE Bonus

Introduction

If you have ever wondered how YouTube marketing works, and whether you can actually make money on it, then this is a good guide for you. You may be afraid that YouTube will waste your time. After all, anyone with an internet connection can become a YouTube publisher, but only a small percentage of us make good money. I can tell you right now that I know how to make money on YouTube, and this book will help you grow and monetize your channel.

Passive income from YouTube is actually really easy. There are a few tricks that will 10X your results, but once you learn them, you'll understand exactly how to increase your earnings.

The focus of this guide is to transparently share everything that I know about making cash from YouTube. I spend about four hours per month creating YouTube videos, and net an easy $30,000+ in passive income every year.

What You Will Learn:

- The YouTube Hack that siphons thousands of visitors per month, for FREE.
- How to crack the YouTube algorithm for easy rankings
- Looking like a PRO with 10 minute improvements
- How to get a "job replacing" income with a few hours/month

Chapter 1 – The YouTube Opportunity

You get it, right?

By 2017, Cisco estimates that 67% of web traffic will be video content. Not only are videos much easier to create than long-winded articles, they're also consumed with a higher retention rate.

Most people don't read…

Other than Facebook, Twitter, Tumblr, etc., most visitors will spend only a few seconds on text-based content before clicking the "back" button, or moving on to something else (likely a video).

Video, on the other hand, retains visitors for longer. And in general, is much easier at getting traffic in the first place. Even though articles are quickly losing their grasp on visitor attention, there are also many more articles on the inter-webs than videos.

In other words, less videos are getting a LOT more traffic.

Convinced yet?

What do I know about making videos?

In the last 30 days, my YouTube videos have been seen over 72,000 times.

This is not to brag. But creating only 80 videos, and receiving that kind of traffic, would be unheard of with a comparable amount of articles. That's almost a thousand sets of eyeballs per video (on average).

Not to mention, these views are all in the highly competitive "make money online" space.

Even better results (numbers-wise) could be had in LOADS of other niches.

What can you do with video traffic?

You have lots of options with video.

You can:

- Collect leads
- Make affiliate sales
- AdSense revenue
- Branding
- Website promotion

Pretty much anything you can do with a blog, you can do with a video.

Chapter 2 – How to Create your Videos

Making videos is easy. To start, you have a few options.

- Talking head
- Slideshow
- Screen Capture

A brief explanation of each:

1) Talking Head- Person(s) in front of a camera. Discussing a niche-related topic.
2) Slideshow- A series of slides or animations with a voice over.
3) Screen Capture- the speaker records screen while giving instructions.

In my opinion, the video style you choose should depend on your niche.

My favourite, and the style I use the most, is <u>Slideshow</u> or <u>Screen Capture</u>

A screen recording with voiceover sounds <u>as boring as cats,</u> but with the tools on the market today, you can easily make a *snazzy* looking video that both impresses and earns sales.

People eat these vids up… And with a *step-by-step* format, it's very realistic to get eyeballs to engage and take action on your videos. This is CRUCIAL in making sales.

You can see the screen capture videos I create, right here.

How to create these videos?

You can do this entire stuff 100% for free, and in the next few minutes with a tool called Microsoft Expression Encoder.

You will have some limitations with this tool, though.

First off, you're only able to record 10 minutes max. For many of us – that's a problem.

And it lacks *features* you'll get with a premium tool.

Always got to give a shout out to Microsoft for making Expression Encoder free. Not all of us have a budget to use on a video-editing tool.

If you do have even a tiny amount of cash to invest, then you absolutely should get a premium tool.

What you should buy!

There are dozens of video creation tools on the market. All of them feature their own perks and have their own drawbacks.

The learning curve is <u>very high</u> for most of them.

VideoMakerFX is the video creator that I recommend the most to newbies – because it's easy to use, and creates some *really badass* videos.

Its focus is slideshow vids with cool animations. Take a look here!

This is an especially good option for people that prefer not to show their face on camera. I remember starting my own video creation in the beginning. I refused to show my face – I was too damn shy. This tool would have been a godsend back then.

VideoMakerFX has everything you need, for less than $97…

Here's what you get…

Most other video creators either cost WAYYY Too much money, or offer no online support for their products.

VideoMakerFX offers top-notch online support, and is priced very reasonably.

How many people are using VideoMakerFX?

One concern about software tools (in general) is future updates. The problem with many of these software programs is that once the product creator's made the moola, they have no incentive to keep their customers happy – they move on to the next shiny object.

VideoMakerFX has sold over 29,500 copies… It's not going away. You can confidently expect future updates for many years. You may not realize how important that is… Lots of these video tools come and go… You can have full confidence that this will be here for good.

It's actually the #1 selling product of all-time on JvZoo. Forget the "product of the day" awards. This one's the best seller… Ever!

Okay, okay Brendan…

It's the best seller of all time on JvZoo. Beating out all the other alternatives. That's pretty impressive.

So far, I know that:

- It's easy to use (unlike most alternatives)
- It creates high quality slideshow videos
- It includes background music
- It includes tons of background images
- Also comes with 140+ animation slides

I also know that video is literally the way of the future.

In less than a decade, <u>over 60% of web traffic will be to videos.</u>

So I should create videos, if I want to be successful from here on out.

This is the easiest, and most impressive video tool under $200.

…

==> Grab Your Copy While it's Still on Special <==

You'll be able to throw together simple YouTube vids in the next few minutes.

Chapter 3 – Making the Most from YouTube

The traffic numbers you can get from YouTube is absolutely outrageous!

Right now, I'm getting about 3,100 visitors per day, and it continues to climb every week.

What would you do with that much traffic?

- Redirect them to your blog
- Get email subscribers
- Make affiliate commissions
- Quit your job

With the traffic you can get from YouTube, you could easily make a comfortable living in no time.

HOWEVER

There are a couple things you have to know.

1. Your videos can't be pointless
2. You need to promote them

Your videos are POINTLESS if they do not get more fans to your channel or make you affiliate commissions with product placement.

At the beginning, your priority should be about growing your fan base and getting more views on your videos.

There are TWO main ways to grow your channel

- Email List
- YouTube Organic

Growing an email list (highly recommended) is like having traffic on tap. At any time – send visitors to whatever you want. In other words… having a list could be more like having money on tap.

Of course, you'll send a lot of your email traffic to affiliate promotions, or traffic exchanges. That's where you can make some REAL BIG MOOLA.

Still, sending visitors to video is an excellent opportunity to build trust with your subscribers, while growing your YouTube channel at the same time.

I like to mix in a few video promotions per week to my mailing list. I send emails daily. To get on my list, go here.

I have no real hard data that proves my email-to-video promotions are impactful. These have helped me grow my channel a lot, though. Your email subs are some of your biggest fans. Showing them what you're doing on YouTube is going to be well received by them.

To learn how to grow an email list fast. I have a full step-by-step guide here: How to Build a List Fast

With your email list — you'll have traffic forever!

Growing the Organic Way

YouTube is a search engine, just like Google.com

Getting organic traffic from YouTube is as simple as ranking in their search listings.

OR... an easier way, is to be listed in their related vids sidebar -- more on that later. It's UBER powerful, and is used by the better YouTube marketers.

Let's get back...

Chapter 4 – Cracking the YouTube Algorithm

In order to reach the top spots of YouTube search, you need to impress the YouTube algorithm.

Let's be clear… Google owns YouTube.

That means that the algorithm for YouTube operates the SAME way.

YouTube's algorithm has metrics (things it pays attention to). Get the best #'s on YouTube's metrics, and the top spot is yours. It's that simple.

Let's talk about the metrics!

How YouTube Ranks Videos?

There are 5 main factors for YouTube ranking.

- Optimization – Video title, description, tags, etc.
- Engagement – Likes, shares, comments, embeds, etc.
- Retention – How long viewers are watching…
- Authority – Channel views, subscribers, etc.
- # of Views – Self-explanatory. # of views on the video.

Video optimization is *easy* to master. It's a simple science of picking the search term(s) you want ranked, and then selecting a title and description that focus on that term(s).

Engagement on your vids is important. A simple way to increase your likes, shares and comments is to ask (in-video) for them. Sounds stupidly simple – but it works!

Retention rate is a crucial metric. In short, it's how long your visitors watch your video. Full watch-throughs will improve this metric. Cutting out before midway will seriously impede your video's rank. Retention is life or death. You WILL NOT rank without a good score.

There are a few tricks to improve retention. In general, though, the quality of your video matters most. Videos that use humor, curiosity, or legitimately stimulate viewers will usually have higher retention rates.

Authority is a reward to channel owners that consistently create high retention videos. This will not be granted overnight – it's a growing gift that increases as you publish more quality videos. My channel started with zero authority – now my videos get ranked much more easily than before.

# of views is much easier when you already have ranked videos or channel authority. Without the luxury of having an established channel, you'll have to work a bit harder to get this one improved. Sharing videos on social networks or mailing to your list are two great ways to get more views. Something to think about…

Those are the 5 main factors in YouTube's algorithm. The last two are usually going to take some time for new YouTubers — the first three are what you should focus on.

Getting your videos ranked organically is a lot of free traffic.

Once you have an established YouTube channel (like mine), organic rankings will come a lot easier.

Chapter 5 – Keyword Research

This is the same as finding keywords for a blog post. Your best bet is to use Google Keyword Planner, or if you have some spare change, invest in LongTailPro.

I created keyword research tutorials here, here and here.

… Let's start from scratch, though. This'll be quick.

Go to Google Keyword Planner.

Click on the button shown in the image below.

Once you click on "Search for new keywords…"

You'll get this drop down.

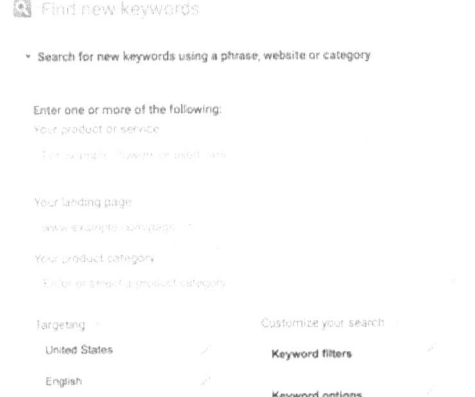

Now you just need to fiddle around for a few minutes and find some seed keyword ideas.

Examples of seed keywords:

- Affiliate marketing
- Link building
- Get traffic
- Create a blog
- Keyword research

Once you get your seed keywords, now plug them into <u>YouTube search</u> and see what results pop up.

For example…

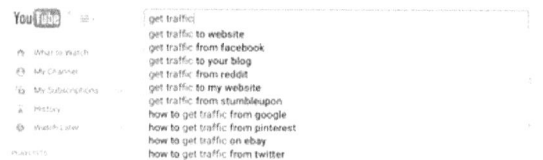

From this quick method – I can see a few GREAT keyword opportunities.

- Get Traffic to Your Blog
- Get Traffic from Reddit
- Get Traffic to My Website
- How to Get Traffic from Google

There is a SIMPLE method to getting more views. Even for high authority channels. I'm about to share the #1 best way to get video views — it's not organic search.

Chapter 6 – YouTube Siphon Hack

There is a traffic source that trumps organic search. It's called "suggested videos," and it can be massive.

Here's a look at my YouTube traffic sources.

My traffic from suggested videos almost DOUBLES YouTube search. And that's analytics from a channel with a dozen or so ranked videos. As a newbie, suggested videos are even MORE important. This is your video goldmine.

What can you do to get more Suggested Views?

Do a quick YouTube search for relevant keywords. <– Do not worry about organic search competition. With this method, we are not trying to rank our video. We are getting our video to show up on the right sidebar for videos that are already ranking.

For example…

Let's say we decided on the keyword "how to make money with YouTube"

Here are the videos that are currently ranking:

You'll notice:

- The #1 ranked video has over 800,000 views.
- The #2 ranked video has over 350,000 views.

We're not going to try and outrank these videos. Maybe one day… But right now, these are exceptionally high quality videos created by channels that have WAYY more authority than ours!

Instead, we want to be the video that shows up on the sidebar for one of these videos.

Like this:

How To Make Money On YouTube (4 Simple Strategies)

I put a red circle around one of the suggested vids.

Notice how most of these sidebar videos have 700,000+ views…

That's almost (and in some cases, more) views than the top ranked video.

Clearly, getting to the top spots of these suggested videos is very valuable.

How to do it!

The algorithm for suggested videos is very simple.

- Video Similarity
- Video Quality

There are a few other factors – but these are the main two.

Video Similarity is the <u>MOST</u> important factor. We're going to maximize our chance of getting suggested traffic by making our video as similar as possible to already ranking videos.

In other words…

We're going to find out:

- The title of ranking videos
- The description
- A brief look at the video content
- Lastly, the tags of the video

Then, we're going to optimize our video's title, description, content and tags. So that it's very close – but different – to the ranking video.

Let's look at the top ranking video again…

The first three factors are easy to find and emulate. <u>Video Tags</u> are a little harder to uncover – they're the secret sauce to claiming your spot, though. So pay attention!

Title = How to Make Money on YouTube (4 Simple Strategies)

Description = In this video, James Wedmore discusses the FOUR simple strategies for actually monetizing your efforts on YouTube.com. However, even though James mentions FOUR strategies, he only recommends one…the last one… (Continued…)

Content = James is talking about 4 strategies that you can use to make money from YouTube.

Video Tags = I bolded the title of "video tags" cause this is easily the most important of the bunch. You've probably heard at one point or another that tags are insignificant. That may be true when it comes to Google Search – YouTube's algorithm is different. It relies on video tags to understand what the video is about…

Why is this the case?

Google spiders cannot enter videos. It's a geeky story – just trust me, though. Google spiders can easily whip through text-based content in no time. When a G-bot runs into a video, it skips over it, and looks at any other indicators to decide the content.

So video tags are literally a conversation piece to the YouTube algorithm. You're telling it exactly what your video is all about. This is where you want to have to tags similar to our target video.

How to Find Video Tags

The easiest way to find YouTube tags is to use this chrome extension.

Here's the step-by-step:

- Open up Google Chrome (or download it)
- Go to http://vidiq.com/apps/vision/
- Go to YouTube and pick video to uncover tags
- Make sure you're logged into Vision
- Video Tags on right sidebar

If you completed this process, you should see a box that looks like this…

Pretty cool, huh?

These are the video tags for the #1 ranking video on "How to Make Money on YouTube"

My advice is to copy <u>60% of these tags</u> and paste them unchanged into your video.

Then find another similar video with a good amount of views, and copy 20%-50% of its tags.

Finally, create 5-10 original tags, one of which is your channel name (more on this later...)

By simply focusing on:

- Similar tags
- Descriptions
- Title
- Content

You are increasing your chance of being the #1 suggested vid

When you go to YouTube, how many videos do you watch?

Chances are, you watch more than one video. The suggested video sidebar gets used ALL THE TIME.

The slogan for YouTube, could easily be "bet ya can't watch just one"

The average user watches <u>3+ videos</u> on EACH session.

That's why it's so powerful to have your video in the sidebar.

One More Advanced U-Tube Trick for even MORE Traffic

There's one more way to use video tags to get more traffic.

Take a look here:

How to Create a Niche Site? (60 Mins to Profit)

This is one of my videos on How to Create a Video Niche Site

For what I'm about to show you – I could have chosen ANY of my videos.

Basically, you want to create a tag for ALL of your videos that is UNIQUE to YOU.

The tag I use is "Brendan Mace"

You'll notice that I have THREE suggested videos above the fold. That's more than half of all videos showing in the sidebar.

Really simple:

- My video showing includes my unique tag: "Brendan Mace"
- My suggested videos also include tag: "Brendan Mace"

For every video I create, I include this tag. This increases the odds of YouTube including MY VIDEOS in the suggested sidebar.

So if the average user watches 3+ videos in a single session. There is a damn good chance they'll watch 2+ of my videos, if they view a vid on my channel.

Pretty cool, huh?

Those two advanced YouTube marketing secrets alone have OUTRAGEOUSLY increased my popularity.

If I can do it – so can you!

Chapter 7 – Making Cash

You can get all the traffic in the world, but you won't make a penny without monetizing it.

The easiest form of monetization also happens to be the least lucrative.

Monetizing with AdSense – Should you do it?

To make money with AdSense on YouTube – All you have to do is become a YouTube Partner and activate ads on all your videos.

This one's tough… Most marketers are on one side of the fence, or the other.

James Wetmore claims that AdSense monetization is a waste, and there are more lucrative ways to make money from YouTube videos.

That's 100% true. There are better ways to make FAT STACKS from YouTube.

The question is… Should you do both?

I use YouTube AdSense for a several hundred-dollar income stream (not allowed to reveal any exact figures).

I make WAYY more with product placement links. I'm happy with some extra hundreds every month, though. In the end, it's all up to you!

Making the Real FAT STACKS on YouTube – What Most are Missing!

The best way to make money with YouTube is actually a fairly untapped strategy. It's using in-video annotations to direct traffic to affiliate products.

Be CAREFUL!

There's a good way to do this…

Take a look at this video.

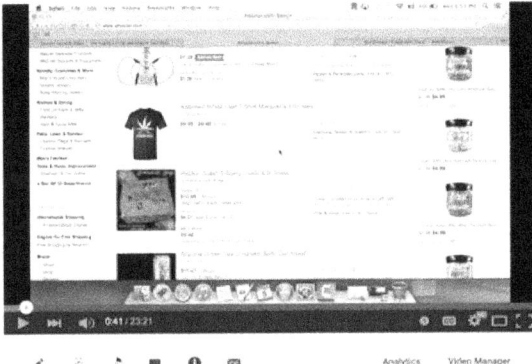

Create a Profitable Niche Site In 20 Mins (Covert Theme)

In this video, I shared a full 23-minute tutorial on how to create a niche site

Watch the video – you'll notice the promotion complements the tutorial.

You want to give away LOADS of value for two reasons.

1 Your vids will not be considered spammy
2 Your vids will get WAYY more exposure (people will actually share them)

Most marketers get a little lazy here, and tell viewers to click a link in the description.

That's an all right strategy – you will make some sales.

The BETTER option is to have video annotations.

Your CTR is WAYY higher with in-video annotation. Lemme show ya how to do that.

How to Create In-Video Annotations – For MAX CTR

First off – you need to actually be a YouTube partner to use annotations. Which is valuable for many reasons. Become one ASAP!

— I created a video on how to do this —="_blank">Try watching this video on www.youtube.com</a>, or enable JavaScript if it is disabled in your browser.

Getting annotations for your videos is UBER important. Be sure to do this – your results will be much better.

The one question you likely have at this point… is so what, annotations can only be sent to associated website links.

Ahhhhhhh…

Good question – you're 100% right.

Annotations can only link to your site – we have a nice little workaround, though…

To direct traffic to affiliate products, or anything for that matter – you just need to create redirect links on your website.

A good tool for this is called PrettyLink

The Lite Version (which is all you need) can host links on your site that direct to ANY address you want.

Cool eh?

So for example…

You could have a link on your site that's www.yoursite.com/anything

That link could *technically* be hosted by your site – but will redirect anywhere you want.

And that's EXACTLY how you get away with sending traffic from annotations to anywhere you want.

What Does YouTube Think About This?

They're fine with it. There are many YouTube publishers that use this exact strategy to get traffic to where they want. It's 100% TOS compliant.

However!

YouTube does care about "low quality content" that's SOLELY created to get visitors to affiliate links.

This is, again, where my insistence on quality videos is important.

With high quality videos, YouTube is happy to help you be successful.

You want to work with YouTube – not against them.

Chapter 8 – Nuggets of Wisdom

Remember earlier we discussed the importance of video engagement and views.

How many times your video is embedded and/or shared on FB and Twitter has an impact on your video rankings.

Here's a list of what YouTube looks for….

77.9 Views Per Hour	**3.2M** Minutes Watched	**826.2K** Views
38 Embedded Sources	**80.8K** Channel Subscribers	**434** Youtube Shares 0.1% of views
5,872 Subscribers Driven 0.7% of views	**106** FB Likes 0.0% of views	**242** FB Shares 0.0% of views
45 FB Comments 0.0% of views	**11K** YouTube Likes	**1,388** YouTube Dislikes
300 Tweets 0.0% of views	**3,673** Google +1's	**1** StumbleUpon Views 0.0% of views
3 LinkedIn Count	**10** Desc Link Count	**235** Desc Word Count
156.5 Words Per Minute	**1/19** Creator Suggested	**2.0%** True Engagement Rate

Includes lots of social behavior:

FB likes/comments, Tweets, Google +1's, YouTube shares/likes.

… And Embeds.

Hmmmmmm…

How can we get this ball rolling?

Embeds are where you share the video on another website.

It's easy – Copy the embed code and enter the code into another site.

It looks like this:

When you embed the video on your site, it'll show up as a full YouTube video, hosted on your website.

Not only will you get extra video views (a ranking factor), it'll also count as an embed source (also a ranking factor).

So TWO ranking boosts, all in one go…

Pretty damn cool.

Where else can we embed our vids?

I like to create video niche sites where I publish ALL my YouTube videos.

They look like this one here: http://macevidz.com

Every single one of my videos gets an additional embed – as well as shares, views, etc.

The theme I use for this is called CovertVideoPress

I love this theme for the embeds – but it's also exceptional at getting FB likes and social shares.

Here's a quick look:

Take a look at the bottom left…

There's a "like" and "share" button.

These work because they're located right where YouTube's like and share buttons would be…

Except in this case, visitors like the video on FACEBOOK instead of YouTube.

Which will also work to distribute the video to all their friends.

And get even more exposure to your video(s).

Where else can we share?

Another great option is on all your social networks.

Facebook, Pinterest, Twitter, Tumblr, Social Blogs, Etc.

With most of these networks, you just need to post the URL of the video, and they'll take care of the code for you.

This will get ya an extra embed – and with some FB friends, you could even get a few Facebook likes and views.

Here's an example:

Easy, right?

That's a simple way to boost your traffic and shares.

Cheap Outsourcing for Quicker Results – Fiverr is Your Friend

Fiverr is a site that sells things for $5.

There are a few things you should buy that will REALLY ramp things up.

- Video intro
- Video outro
- Channel art
- Video thumbnails
- Social bookmarks

A video intro and channel art is an important professional touch.

When viewers check out your channel – they are way more likely to subscribe if you're channel looks like a million bucks.

All in – channel art and a video intro will cost ya 10 bucks.

There's NO REASON to skip this step. It's the cheapest way to add a TON of subscribers and views to your bottom line.

Go to Fiverr and search for "video intro" and "YouTube header"

A video outro is important for three reasons:

1 Looks professional
2 Subscriber collector
3 Related views

Similar to the intro, it's a nice touch to your videos.

It ALSO has the function of getting more subscribers and related views.

Here's a look at my outro:

It includes links to other videos on my channel.

Most importantly – it has the "Subscribe" button.

These are all connected to video annotations. So when visitors click on the buttons, they actually perform the appropriate tasks.

This is an awesome way to collect a bunch of extra leads and views.

You should do this!

Video thumbnails are crucial for more views

Part of the YouTube algorithm (not yet discussed) is CTR.

When your video shows up in search or in the suggested videos, you need people to actually CLICK on the thumbnail of your video.

By default, YouTube will take a snapshot of the middle of your video, and use it as the thumbnail.

The better option is to submit a custom thumbnail.

You could make this yourself.

Cause I'm lazy – and want it done professionally. I spend… you guessed it… $5 to get all my thumbnails done on Fiverr.

Check them out here: Brendan Mace's YouTube Channel

All those thumbnails cost me $5 a piece.

That's a steal – in my opinion.

Social bookmarks will boost your YouTube and Google rankings.

You could do social bookmarking all manually.

OR, you could get hundreds of bookmarks for $5.

For example:

A few hundred social bookmarks will improve your video seo.

Social bookmarks are optional – these can all be earned manually.

Adding some additional one's through Fiverr is not a bad idea, though.

And cheap!

Conclusion

Here's a quick look at my YouTube stats (last 30 days)

Performance

VIEWS
86,413

ESTIMATED MINUTES WATCHED
336,625

Engagement

LIKES	DISLIKES	COMMENTS	SHARES
621	73	421	211

In the last month – 336,626 minutes = 234 days worth of viewing time.

Imagine how many sales you could make with that viewing time.

It's easy:

- Get VideoMakerFX to create videos
- Optimize your videos for engagement
- Pick the right keywords
- Use video tags to steal competitors traffic
- Video annotations for maximum sales
- Embed videos on other sites/networks
- Use Fiverr for cheap, professional designs

That's everything I know about video marketing. My YouTube channel makes me about $2k/month on complete autopilot.

Once you have this stuff up and running – you can relax.

Travel the world. Live your life!

Passive income has always been the goal for me. Creating a growing YouTube channel with all the sneaky tricks and embellishments can give you the life of your dreams.

Remember – I'm here to help. Living in Medellin, Colombia – helping as many of my followers as possible achieve the laptop lifestyle. You could be next!

Wrapping Up

I hope you enjoyed reading about my simple two-step formula.

My last piece of advice is this: Don't let _small minds_ convince you that your dreams are TOO BIG. You can do this!!

If you would like to learn more about how to build passive income online, then I would love to chat with you. Check out my blog that shares in depth guides, like this one. Right here: www.brendanmace.com

www.ingramcontent.com/pod-product-compliance
Lightning Source LLC
Chambersburg PA
CBHW070223210526
45169CB00024B/1531